TAKE UP THY SWORD - VOL. I
Prayer Guide & Bible Companion

WHEN HEAVEN HEARS YOUR PRAYER

*Then hear thou in heaven their prayer and their
supplication, and maintain their cause.*
1 Kings 8:45

SHARLYNE C. THOMAS

Scripture quotations are from the King James Version
of the Holy Bible unless otherwise indicated.

Cover & Interior Design by Tarsha L. Campbell

DOMINIONHOUSE
Publishing & Design
P.O. Box 681938
Orlando, FL 32868
(407) 880-5790 phone/fax
www.mydominionhouse.com

*The Lord gave the word: great was the company of those
that published it (Psalm 68:11).*

DEDICATION

This book is dedicated to my lovely daughter, Cierra Danyelle. Thank you for sharing me with the body of Christ so I can be about my heavenly Father's business. I pray that you will always have that sweet spirit while maturing into a Mighty Woman of God who will speak the Word with boldness and confidence.

"Blessed be thou of the Lord, my daughter"
(Ruth 3:10).

CONTACT INFORMATION

Sharlyne C. Thomas
cb_tp@yahoo.com **or** carmone73104@bellsouth.net

Please feel free to email the author with any comments you may have. You are also welcome to contact her for bookings. She is available for book club presentations, signings, or speaking engagements for your church or organization (i.e. ministry or club events, workshops, conferences, retreats, and seminars).

TABLE OF CONTENTS

...But if any man be a worshipper of God, and doeth His will, him He heareth (John 9:31).

INTRODUCTION

Do you ever feel as though your prayers are hitting a glass ceiling and you're not being heard? Or maybe the answers are not arriving as fast as you'd like or not at all? The disciples said to Jesus in Luke 11:1, *"Lord, teach us to pray"*. If we want to ensure that God truly hears us when we call, then we have to know <u>how</u> to pray – there is a strategy for getting results. We also need the faith and endurance to stand on the Word and wait for that still, small voice to lead the way. My prayer for you is that this book will provide the tools and encouragement that you need to reach Heaven's ear by coming to the Father's throne in the name of Jesus Christ, *in whom we have boldness and access with confidence by the faith of Him* (Ephesians 3:12). According to James 5:16, *the effectual fervent prayer of a righteous man availeth much*; so when you learn how to pray earnestly as shown in verse 17 of the same chapter, that is WHEN HEAVEN HEARS YOUR PRAYER!

And if we know that He hear us, whatsoever we ask, we know that we have the petitions that we desired of Him (1 John 5:15).

PART I

GOD IS LISTENING

Have you ever been frustrated during a conversation or argument because you felt like the other person wasn't listening to you? I have thought to myself many times before, "I'm not even going to waste my breath"! It's not fun to feel like you're talking to a brick wall. Fortunately we serve a God whose ear is not heavy *that it cannot hear* (Isaiah 59:1). And according to Psalm 121:4, *he that keepeth Israel shall neither slumber nor sleep* - that means you can reach Him <u>anytime</u>. The Lord sits patiently on His throne waiting for us to call upon His holy name – not just when we need or want something, but all the time. In order to have true intimacy with God, we need to keep constant, two-way communication. David tells us in Psalm 145:18-19:

The Lord is nigh unto all them that call upon him, to all that call upon him in truth. He will fulfill the desire of them that fear him: he also will hear their cry, and will save them.

The Father does hear our cries. In First Chronicles 28:9, we learn that God can also hear our <u>thoughts</u>. He told Isaiah in chapter 66, verse 18, that *"I know their works and their thoughts"*. I can tell you first-hand that these scriptures are true. About two years ago, I would usually wear jeans to church just to be comfortable after dressing up for work all week long. One day while getting ready for church, I simply thought to myself (not in a prayer directed at the Lord) how nice it will be when I can finally afford to wear "church suits" every Sunday. That very morning, a Mighty Woman of God that I would sometimes sit by just asked me, "So, what size are you?". The next week without any effort or request on my part, this woman and another friend of hers blessed me with 18 beautiful, like-new church suits (all varieties)! I was in shock, to say the least - God had actually answered a prayer that I innocently thought was just a private wish. Surely we can all proclaim, *"He that is mighty hath done to me great things"* (Luke 1:49)!

If ye have faith... (Matthew 21:21).

We have to reach that point in our faith where we can say like Jesus, *"Father, I thank thee that thou hast heard me. And I knew that thou hearest me always"* (John 11:41-42). In Psalm 65:2, David also shows complete faith in God and refers to Him as *"Thou that hearest prayer"*. We don't want to be like Zacharias in the first chapter of Luke whose mouth was shut for the duration of Elizabeth's pregnancy with John the Baptist due to his lack of faith. God sent His archangel (Gabriel) to tell Zacharias that his prayer for a son was heard, but he couldn't look past his current circumstances and focus on the future promise. How can we doubt God's Word when Second Corinthians 5:7 tells us that *we walk by faith, not by sight?* We must remember that *the things which are seen are temporal, but the things which are not seen are eternal* (2 Corinthians 4:18). Don't let what you see in the natural discourage you from believing that it hasn't already come to pass "in the spirit". Faith, which is the opposite of fear, is the key! When we pray, we must have the faith to believe that our prayers have been heard and will be answered. Jesus told his disciples in Mark 11:22-24:

Have in faith in God. For verily I say unto you, That whosoever shall say unto this mountain, Be thou removed, and be thou cast into the sea; and shall not doubt in his heart, but shall believe that those things which he saith shall come to pass; he shall have whatsoever he saith. Therefore I say unto you, What things soever ye desire when ye pray, believe that ye receive them, and ye shall have them.

Jesus told his disciples in Luke 17:6 that *faith as a grain of mustard seed* is all that's necessary for even a tree to obey you! Now stop for a moment and try to imagine how small that seed really is. May I assume that your faith is larger than that? If you said "yes", then *nothing shall be impossible unto you* (Matthew 17:20).

The eleventh chapter of Hebrews is usually referred to as "the faith chapter". Verse 1 tells us that *faith is the substance of things hoped for, the evidence of things not seen.* But perhaps the most important verse to remember in this chapter is that *without faith it is impossible to please Him* (Hebrews 11:6)! The Apostle Paul reminds us in Romans 8:25 that *if we hope for that we see not, then do we with patience wait for it.* We must believe that God both hears and answers our prayers - even if the promise seems delayed or wrapped in a different package than we expected. You may have to say like the desperate father crying out for his son in Mark 9:24, *"Lord, I believe; help thou mine unbelief".* Whether you have a major problem or a simple issue, remember what Jesus told his disciples: *Whatsoever ye shall ask the Father in my name, he will give it you* (John 16:23).

Ask ye of the Lord... (Zechariah 10:1).

How can we complain about not having something, or someone, if we have not yet asked for it? James answers this question in chapter 4, verse 2, when he says that *ye have not because ye ask not.* So now you say, "but I <u>have</u> asked"! O.k. then, let's go back to James 1:6-7:

> *But let him ask in faith, nothing wavering. For he that wavereth is like a wave of the sea driven with the wind and tossed. For let not that man think that he shall receive any thing of the Lord.*

We need to believe that whatever we have prayed for has already been done before we say, "Amen"! We serve a loving, faithful God who <u>does</u> hear and answer prayer. Remember Martha, the sister of Lazarus? In the eleventh chapter of John, she found the strength and courage to believe the Word of the Lord - even in the midst of her own brother's death! Martha said to Jesus in verse 22, *"But I know, that even now, whatsoever thou wilt ask of God, God will give it thee".* Lazarus was raised from the dead for the glory of God <u>and</u> because of the faithful prayers of Martha. And Jesus reminds us again in John 14:13-14 that *whatsoever ye shall ask in my name, that will I do, that the Father may be glorified in the Son. If ye shall ask any thing in my name, I will do it.*

When your children ask you for certain things (especially if it's simple and/or inexpensive), don't you usually say, "O.k., honey"? If a close friend asks for a ride to church, wouldn't you say, "Sure, no problem"? Well... *how much more shall your Father which is in Heaven give good things to them that ask Him*

13

(Matthew 7:11)? Just before that scripture, Jesus told his disciples in verses 7-8: *Ask, and it shall be given you; seek, and ye shall find; knock, and it shall be opened unto you: For every one that asketh receiveth; and he that seeketh findeth; and to him that knocketh it shall be opened.* And our Father actually tells us in Isaiah 45:11, *concerning the work of My hands <u>command</u> ye Me!* Of course that doesn't mean that you can boss Him around or treat Him like your personal genie. God just wants us to know that we are entitled to all of the promises in His Word if we are willing and obedient according to Isaiah 1:19.

We learned in First Samuel 15:22 that *to obey is better than sacrifice, and to hearken than the fat of rams.* Aren't you glad that we live under the new covenant which does not require the killing of any animals to get God's attention? Neither do we have to perform any religious ceremony to enter into His presence. When I wanted to know where God planned to use me at my church, I just simply asked Him during one service - and not even out loud! That same afternoon at a friend's barbecue, she said to me: "Oh, yeah - the Holy Spirit told me to tell you to join the prayer ministry". At that point in my salvation and deliverance process, I had no idea what a "Prayer Warrior" was, but I made the choice to be obey His voice. During my first three years in that small chapel, the Word was poured into me so much that it can now flow <u>out</u> of me like *rivers of living water* (John 7:38).

Part I - God is Listening

When you ask the Lord for direction and obey His instructions, then you can join me in declaring, *"I will praise His Word"* (Psalm 56:4)!

However if you're walking in disobedience, then you're hindering your own prayers. Isaiah 59:2 states that *your iniquities have separated between you and your God, and your sins have hid His face from you, that He will not hear!* Each blessing comes with a condition as illustrated in John 15:7 when Jesus said, *"If ye abide in Me, and My words abide in you, ye shall ask what ye will, and it shall be done unto you."* And we're reminded again in 1 John 3:22 that *whatsoever we ask, we receive of Him, because we keep His commandments, and do those things that are pleasing in His sight.* The Lord clearly reveals the rewards for obedience and the consequences for disobedience in the twenty-eighth chapter of Deuteronomy. Although there could be a variety of reasons for an unanswered prayer, we need to look in the mirror first before we attempt to blame our Father for our own "undesirable" circumstances.

God is not a man that He should lie... (Numbers 23:19).

Believe what is written in the scriptures. God is listening! Whenever you need to encourage yourself in the Lord, like David in First Samuel 30:6, just meditate on the Word:

And the Lord said unto him, I have heard thy prayer and thy supplication, that thou hast made before me... (1 Kings 9:3).

But know that the Lord hath set apart him that is godly for Himself: the Lord will hear when I call unto Him (Psalm 4:3).

Lord, thou hast heard the desire of the humble: thou wilt prepare their heart, thou wilt cause Thine ear to hear (Psalm 10:17).

I have called upon thee, for thou wilt hear me, O God: incline thine ear unto me, and hear my speech (Psalm 17:6).

Now know I that the Lord saveth His anointed; He will hear him from His holy Heaven with the saving strength of His right hand (Psalm 20:6).

Blessed be the Lord, because he hath heard the voice of my supplications (Psalm 28:6).

He shall call upon Me, and I will answer him: I will be with him in trouble; I will deliver him, and honour him (Psalm 91:15).

The Lord is far from the wicked: but he heareth the prayer of the righteous (Proverbs 15:29).

Then shalt thou call, and the Lord shall answer; thou shalt cry, and He shall say, Here I am... (Isaiah 58:9).

PART I - GOD IS LISTENING

And it shall come to pass, that before they call, I will answer; and while they are yet speaking, I will hear (Isaiah 65:24).

Then shall ye call upon Me, and ye shall go and pray unto Me, and I will hearken unto you (Jeremiah 29:12).

Therefore I will look unto the Lord; I will wait for the God of my salvation: my God will hear me (Micah 7:7).

And the inhabitants of one city shall go to another, saying, Let us go speedily to pray before the Lord, and to seek the Lord of hosts: I will go also (Zechariah 8:21).

PART II

WORD POWER

Now that you know God is listening, what will you say? Paul tells us in First Thessalonians 5:17 to *pray without ceasing*; and in First Timothy 2:1 that *supplications, prayers, intercessions, and giving of thanks be made for all men*. A prayer is simply a conversation with God - that means both talking <u>and</u> listening. There are different types of prayer, including intercession - when you pray (or sometimes "travail") on behalf of another. In the Bible, you will frequently see "supplications" and prayers being made to the Father. A supplication is when you're making a special plea or urgent request. These are usually the "on-your-knees-in-desperate-need-of-help" prayers. Whether you're asking the Lord to do something for you or thanking Him for what He's already done, there are proven techniques for productive prayer.

...Where is the word of the Lord? let it come now (Jeremiah 17:15).

In order to send up to Heaven an *effectual fervent prayer of a righteous man [that] availeth much* (James 5:16), we need to pray the Word of God. Paul explains to us in Second Timothy 3:16 that *all scripture is given by inspiration of God, and is profitable for doctrine, for reproof, for correction, for instruction in righteousness.* Do you know why the angels are *hearkening unto the voice of His Word* as recorded in Psalm 103:20? We can find the answer in John 1:1, 14:

In the beginning was the Word, and the Word was with God, and the Word was God...And the Word was made flesh, and dwelt among us...

So what do you think would reach God's ears faster - our murmuring and complaining, or His own Word (Jesus Christ) that is *quick, and powerful, and sharper than any twoedged sword* (Hebrews 4:12)? We learned that in the midst of Daniel's prayer, the archangel Gabriel said to him, *"thy words were heard, and I am come for thy words"(Daniel 10:12).* What kind of words do you want the angels to take up to Heaven on your behalf?

20

PART II - WORD POWER

We're reminded in Matthew 4:4 that *man shall not live by bread alone, but by every Word that proceedeth out of the mouth of God.* And when Jesus was tempted by the devil in the fourth chapter of Luke, He proclaimed: *"It is <u>written</u>"!* We must put our faith and trust in God, because He said that *[My Word] shall not return unto Me void, but it shall accomplish that which I please, and it shall prosper in the thing whereto I sent it* (Isaiah 55:11). He also tells us in Jeremiah 1:12, *"I will hasten my Word to perform it"* - that means He's watching over His Word to make sure that it is fulfilled in the earth as it is in Heaven.

Sometimes it's hard for us to comprehend the true power of words. For example, God describes His Word as a "fire" and a "hammer" in Jeremiah 23:29. That may be hard to imagine, but just think back to the first chapter of Genesis - God created the entire universe in six days just by <u>speaking</u> it into existence ("And God said...")! Our Lord is so awesome that His Word *shall stand forever* (Isaiah 40:8), and it *shall not pass away* (Matthew 24:35). So what about the power of our words? Because we are made in the image and likeness of our heavenly Father according to Genesis 1:26, and *death and life are in the power of the tongue* (Proverbs 18:21), Jesus warns us about speaking negative words in Matthew 12:34-37:

O generation of vipers, how can ye, being evil, speak good good things? for out of the abundance of the heart the mouth speaketh. A good man out of the good treasure of the heart bringeth forth good things: and an evil man out of the evil treasure bringeth forth evil things. But I say unto you, That every idle word that men shall speak, they shall give account thereof in the day of judgment. For by thy words thou shalt be justified, and by thy words thou shalt be condemned.

...If we ask anything according to His will, He heareth us (1 John 5:14).

Jesus was obedient (even unto death) by saying to the Father in Luke 22:42, *"not my will, but thine, be done"*. So how do we know that we're praying God's perfect will for our lives as opposed to our own permissive will? Since Christ is "The Living Word", then we know that we are submitting to <u>His</u> will when we pray the scriptures. And because *we know not what we should pray for as we ought* according to Romans 8:26, Paul tells us in verse 27 of the same chapter that the Holy Spirit *maketh intercession for the saints according to the will of God*. This can be described as speaking in tongues.

Can you picture the day of Pentecost and those "tongues of fire"? Acts 2:4 states that *they were all filled with the Holy Ghost, and began to speak with other tongues, as the Spirit gave them utterance.* Speaking in tongues - our personal, heavenly prayer language - is a gift of the Spirit and should be used often. First Corinthians 14:2 states that *he that speaketh in an unknown tongue speaketh not unto men, but unto God.* And Paul gives us

22

these instructions in Ephesians 6:17-18:

> *And take...the sword of the Spirit, which is the word of God: Praying always with all prayer and supplication <u>in the Spirit</u>, and watching thereunto with all perseverance and supplication for all saints.*

"But how will I know what I'm saying," you ask? If you or those around you do not have the gift of interpretation of tongues as described in First Corinthians 12:10, that's o.k. - <u>God</u> knows exactly what you're saying! We need to pray [and sing] both in the spirit and "with the understanding" (how we normally communicate) according to First Corinthians 14:15. But remember that you're not alone in this task, for *we have an advocate with the Father, Jesus Christ the righteous* (1 John 2:1). So even when we find ourselves too busy or too tired to pray, Paul reminds us in Hebrews 7:25 that our Savior *ever liveth to make intercession* for us!

Hear ye the word which the Lord speaketh unto you... (Jeremiah 10:1)

Has the Lord given you a Word today? Remember, prayer involves both talking and listening. Now why is the second part so much harder than the first part? God gave us two ears but only <u>one</u> mouth! Perhaps we fail to make a conscious effort to *be swift to hear [and] slow to speak* (James 1:19). Since *all have sinned, and*

23

come short of the glory of God (Romans 3:23), I also sometimes struggle with this aspect of my conversation with the Father. We actually have to train ourselves to become better listeners. But bless the name of the Lord, *for He knoweth our frame; He remembereth that we are dust* (Psalm 103:14). And we don't want to miss out on this special promise found in Isaiah 55:3:

> *Incline your ear, and come unto Me: hear, and your soul shall live; and I will make an everlasting covenant with you, even the sure mercies of David.*

Sometimes we just walk right out of our "prayer closet" without letting God say two words to us! Joshua told the children of Israel in chapter 3 and verse 9, *"Come hither, and hear the words of the Lord your God"*. And James tells us in chapter 4 and verse 8 to *draw nigh to God, and He will draw nigh to you*. We may need to get specific instructions from the Lord before we see the manifestation (evidence) of the answer to our prayer. On occasion, *thine ears shall hear a word behind thee, saying, This is the way, walk ye in it* (Isaiah 30:21). You'll be surprised at what the Holy Ghost will reveal to you when you take the time to listen to Him!

Now when you <u>know</u> it's the voice of God, just obey - don't question Him. But also, don't let the serpent beguile (deceive) you like Eve did in the third chapter of Genesis. We were taught in First John 4:1 that we

24

cannot believe every spirit, but that we must *try the spirits whether they are of God*. When (not if) the enemy attempts to deceive or confuse you, just tell him that you *"are not ignorant of his devices"* as Paul tells us in Second Corinthians 2:11. Remember, *be not deceived: evil communications corrupt good manners* (1 Corinthians 15:33).

Have you already learned how to tune out the world and tune into the Kingdom? You may hear people say, "don't be so heavenly-minded that you're no earthly good"; but don't be discouraged or distracted - find that balance. We all know that *faith cometh by hearing, and hearing by the Word of God* (Romans 10:17). That means not only listening to God when He speaks to our spirit, but we also need to listen to the scriptures via pastors, fellow saints and inspirational media. Because God's Word is *a lamp unto [our] feet, and a light unto [our] path* (Psalm 119:105), we must hear and receive all the words that He speaks to us according to Ezekiel 3:10. As recorded in the Gospels, don't let the fertilized seed of the voice of God fall by the way side, upon stony places or among thorns. Receive His Word into the "good ground" of your heart as Jesus taught us in Matthew 13:23:

But he that received seed into the good ground is he that heareth the Word, and understandeth it; which also beareth fruit, and bringeth forth, some an hundred-fold, some sixty, some thirty.

...Go in unto the king, to make supplication unto him, and to make request before him... (Esther 4:8).

PART III

THIS IS THE DAY

This is the day to see the <u>King</u> of kings! All day, every day, we must *come boldly unto the throne of grace, that we may obtain mercy, and find grace to help in time of need* (Hebrews 4:16). We all lead busy (sometimes hectic) lives; and we may find ourselves so caught up in the things of this world, that we forget to acknowledge our Father and invite Him into every aspect of our day. Remember that the Lord is so awesome, *even the very hairs of your head are all numbered* (Luke 12:7)! Surely He's concerned about the smallest details of our day, and that's why it's so important to keep an "open dialogue" with Him. Because *ye know not what shall be on the morrow* (James 4:14), learn how to pray to Him today.

Like many believers, I didn't know that there is a certain protocol (set of rules) for effective prayer. When I was bound by the chains of religion (as opposed to "relationship"), I prayed constantly - but from the wrong perspective and to the wrong "person". I had to learn that I was seated *together in heavenly places in Christ Jesus* (Ephesians 2:6). I had to start taking my authority and dominion according to Genesis 1:26, and *calleth those things which be not as though they were* (Romans 4:17). I was also taught to pray <u>to</u> our heavenly Father, <u>in</u> the name of Jesus Christ, <u>by</u> the power of the Holy Spirit. Jesus also gave us these instructions in Matthew 6:6-8:

> *But thou, when thou prayest, enter into thy closet, and when thou hast shut thy door, pray to thy Father which is in secret; and thy Father which seeth in secret shall reward thee openly. But when ye pray, use not vain repetitions, as the heathen do: for they think that they shall be heard for their much speaking. Be not ye therefore like unto them: for your Father knoweth what things ye have need of, before ye ask Him.*

We can always look to our Lord and Savior as an example of how we should pray. In the seventeenth chapter of John, we see how Jesus prayed for Himself, His disciples, and for all <u>future</u> believers - that's us! In Hebrews 5:7, Paul tells us that Jesus *had offered up prayers and supplications with strong crying and tears unto Him that was able to save him from death, and was heard in that he feared.* The Son reverenced the Father by giving Him all the honor and glory and obeying His commandments as shown in John 12:49-50. Jesus tells us in John 4:24 that *God is a Spirit: and they that worship Him must worship Him in spirit and in truth.* His ancestor, King David, also reminded us to *enter into His gates with thanksgiving and into His courts with praise: be thankful unto Him, and bless His name* (Psalm 100:4). Each day we should declare with the choirs of Heaven in Revelation 7:12:

Saying, Amen: Blessing, and glory, and wisdom, and thanksgiving, and honour, and power, and might, be unto our God for ever and ever. Amen.

Watch ye therefore, and pray always... (Luke 21:36)

James 1:22 states that we should *be doers of the Word, and not hearers only.* So what should we <u>do</u> each day? Here's one suggestion: *pray that ye enter not into temptation* (Luke 22:40)! We're all tempted by sin on a daily basis, and *if we say that we have not sinned, we make Him a liar, and His Word is not in us* (1 John 1:10). Remember when Jesus told Peter in Luke 22:31, *"Satan hath desired to have you, that he may sift you as wheat"*? Well Saints, <u>we</u> are Satan's target now! And God has already told us that the enemy, *as a roaring lion, walketh about, seeking whom he may devour* (1 Peter 5:8). Therefore, we must always be "prayed-up"! We also received these instructions in First Peter 4:7:

29

But the end of all things is at hand: be ye therefore sober,
and watch unto prayer.

Being "sober" doesn't just mean the opposite of being drunk (but thank God for deliverance); we have to be *of a ready mind* according to First Peter 5:2. As Paul states in Second Timothy 1:7, *God hath not given us the spirit of fear; but of power, and of love, and of a <u>sound mind</u>.* We are made up of three parts - spirit, soul and body. The enemy's main battleground is our mind because that is part of our soul; so we must *continue in prayer, and watch in the same with thanksgiving* (Colossians 4:2). And we have been commanded in Matthew 22:37 to love the Lord with all of our heart, soul and mind. We can keep our mind on Him through continuous prayer (but remember that balance); and if we commit our works unto the Lord, then our *thoughts shall be established* (Proverbs 16:3). And don't forget these encouraging words from Paul in Galatians 6:9 when he said, *"let us not be weary in well doing: for in due season we shall reap, if we faint not"*.

Behold, I give unto you power... over all the power of the enemy... (Luke 10:19).

According to Genesis 3:15, God has put enmity (hatred) between us and Satan. We are here on earth to serve God - not the enemy and not our flesh. We must *be strong and of a good courage* (Joshua 1:6) as we go out to face the world each morning. Decree and declare that *this* is the day which the Lord hath made; we will rejoice and be glad in it* (Psalm 118:24)! Your heavenly Father has not left you alone to fight your daily battles by yourself; for He has promised to be with you and neither fail you nor forsake you as shown in Deuteronomy 31:8.

Did you know that there is also power in <u>numbers</u> when it comes to prayer? Moses explains to us in Deuteronomy 32:30 that because of the Rock of our salvation, one person can chase a 1000 [enemy troops] but two people can put 10,000 to flight! Esther also understood the power of "touching and agreeing" described in Matthew 18:19-20. Let's examine the courage and wisdom in her instructions in Esther 4:16:

Go, gather together all the Jews that are present in Shushan, and fast ye for me, and neither eat nor drink three days, night or day: I also and my maidens will fast likewise; and so will I go in unto the king, which is not according to the law: and if I perish, I perish.

Because of the power of "corporate" prayer and fasting, Esther received favor with the king and the Jews defeated their enemies.

Please don't be afraid of the word "fasting" because you think that you may faint or die from starvation! We need to "die" to our flesh so that we will not fulfill *the desires of the flesh and of the mind* (Ephesians 2:3).

31

Jesus also tells us in Matthew 17:21 that some evil spirits can only be cast out by *prayer and fasting*. The Lord will honor anything that you set aside (such as television) in order to seek Him and to *walk in the Spirit* as described in the fifth chapter of Galatians. Just like Esther, <u>our</u> King will hear and answer our petitions because He *is no respecter of persons* according to Acts 10:34, and He *sendeth rain on the just and on the unjust* (Matthew 5:45). And He will certainly listen when we are gathered, physically or spiritually, with other believers in *one accord in prayer and supplication* (Acts 1:14).

...Those that seek Me early shall find Me
(Proverbs 8:17).

Throughout the whole Bible, we see mighty men and women of God "rising early in the morning". Jesus, Himself, is not excluded from this list as shown in John 8:2 when He got up *early in the morning* to teach the people at the temple. And Mark 1:35 states that *in the morning, rising up a great while before day, He went out, and departed into a solitary place, and there prayed.* Our Savior knew how to lift up His eyes unto the hills and seek His Father like David did in Psalm 121:1. I am definitely not a morning person, but I <u>will</u> get up to pray when the Lord prompts me. Jesus told us in Matthew 6:34 to *take therefore no thought for the morrow,* so we need to be prepared to face the world and the enemy <u>today</u>! So when you hear the Lord calling you as described in the third chapter of First Samuel, just know that He wants to give you a divine task to accomplish. One example of this special assignment is found in Exodus 9:13:

And the Lord said unto Moses, Rise up early in the morning, and stand before Pharaoh, and say unto him, Thus saith the Lord God of the Hebrews, Let my people go, that they may serve me.

According to Second Corinthians 5:20, we are *ambassadors* (representatives) *for Christ;* therefore we have to be attentive when the Father gives us instructions. David said in Psalm 55:17, *Evening, and morning, and at noon, will I pray, and cry aloud: and He shall hear my voice.* He also declared in chapter 101, verse 8, "I will <u>early</u> destroy all the wicked of the land". What gave David the desire and the power to do this? Perhaps it was because in verse 2 of that chapter, he said that he would walk in his house *with a perfect heart.* Clearly, none of us is perfect; but we are being "perfected" according to Ephesians 4:12. That is why we need to cry out to God each morning saying, "Create in me a clean heart, O God; and renew a right spirit within me" (Psalm 51:10). He also wants us to inquire of Him like David did in Psalm 5:2-3:

Hearken unto the voice of my cry, my King, and my God: for unto Thee will I pray. My voice shalt thou hear in the morning, O Lord; in the morning will I direct my prayer unto thee, and will look up.

Paul tells us in Second Corinthians 4:16 that our *inward man is renewed day by day*, so please consider the following prayer essentials as a starting point for your mandatory, daily routine:

The Lord's Prayer

...Our Father which art in Heaven, Hallowed be thy name. Thy kingdom come. Thy will be done in earth, as it is in Heaven. Give us this day our daily bread. And forgive us our debts, as we forgive our debtors. And lead us not into temptation, but deliver us from evil: For thine is the kingdom, and the power, and the glory, for ever. Amen (Matthew 6:9-13).

Praise and Thanksgiving

...Blessed be thou, Lord God of Israel our Father, for ever and ever. Thine, O Lord, is the greatness, and the power, and the glory, and the victory, and the majesty: for all that is in the Heaven and in the earth is thine; thine is the kingdom, O Lord, and thou art exalted as head above all. Both riches and honour come of thee, and thou reignest over all; and in thine hand is power and might; and in thine hand it is to make great, and to give strength unto all. Now therefore, our God, we thank thee, and praise thy glorious name (1 Chronicles 29:10-13).

Repentance

Have mercy upon me, O God, according to thy lovingkindess: according unto the multitude of thy tender mercies blot out my transgressions. Wash me thoroughly from mine iniquity, and cleanse me from my sin. For I acknowledge my transgressions: and my sin is ever before me. Against thee, thee only, have I sinned, and done this evil in thy sight: that thou mightest be justified when thou speakest, and be clear when thou judgest...Purge me with hyssop, and I shall be clean: wash me, and I shall be whiter than snow (Psalm 51:1-4, 7).

Divine Protection
He that dwelleth in the secret place of the most High shall abide under the shadow of the Almighty. I will say of the Lord, He is my refuge and my fortress: my God; in Him will I trust...Because [I have] made the Lord, which is my refuge, even the most High, [my] habitation; There shall no evil befall [me], neither shall any plague come nigh [my] dwelling. For He shall give His angels charge over [me], to keep [me] in all [my] ways. They shall bear [me] up in their hands, lest [I] dash [my] foot against a stone (Psalm 91:1-2, 9-12).

Blessings
And the Lord shall make [me] plenteous in goods, in the fruit of [my] body, and in the fruit of [my] cattle, and in the fruit of [my] ground, in the land which the Lord sware unto [my] fathers to give [me]. The Lord shall open unto [me] His good treasure, the heaven to give the rain unto [my] land in his season, and to bless all the work of [my] hand: and [I] shalt lend unto many nations, and [I] shalt not borrow. And the Lord shall make [me] the head, and not the tail; and [I] shalt be above only, and [I] shalt not be beneath; if that

[I] hearken unto the commandments of the Lord [my] God...
(Deuteronomy 28:11-13).

Armor of God*

[I will] Put on the whole armour of God, that [I] may be able to stand against the wiles of the devil. For we wrestle not against flesh and blood, but against principalities, against powers, against the rulers of the darkness of this world, against spiritual wickedness in high places... [I will] Stand therefore, having [my] loins girt about with truth, and having on the breastplate of righteousness; And [my] feet shod with the preparation of the gospel of peace; Above all, taking the shield of faith, wherewith [I] shall be able to quench all the fiery darts of the wicked. And tak[ing] the helmet of salvation, and the sword of the Spirit, which is the Word of God (Ephesians 6:11-12, 14-17).

Spiritual Warfare*

And there was a war in Heaven: Michael and his angels fought against the dragon; and the dragon fought and his angels, And prevailed not; neither was their place found any more in Heaven. And the great dragon was cast out, that old serpent, called the Devil, and Satan, which deceiveth the whole world: he was cast out into the earth, and his angels were cast out with him. And I heard a loud voice saying in Heaven, Now is come salvation, and strength, and the kingdom of our God, and the power of his Christ: for the accuser of our brethren is cast down, which accused them before our God day and night. And they overcame him by the blood of the Lamb, and by the word of their testimony; and they loved not their lives unto the death...And the devil that deceived them was cast into the lake of fire and brimstone, where the beast and the false prophet are, and shall be tormented day and night for ever and ever (Revelation 12:7-11, 20:10).

*Whenever you prepare for war to bind the enemy and loose the Word as described in Matthew 16:19, you may want to pray while <u>standing</u> in order to *bruise [Satan's] head* (Genesis 3:15). Just ask the Lord to lead you.

...Go in peace: and the God of Israel grant thee thy petition that thou hast asked of Him (1 Samuel 1:17).

PART IV

BRING YOUR PETITIONS

Now that we know 1) God hears our prayer, 2) the power of His Word, and 3) how and why we should pray, Our Father says to us that He *is able to do exceeding abundantly above all that we ask or think, according to the power that worketh in us* (Ephesians 3:20). According to Jeremiah 32:17, there is <u>nothing</u> too hard for God! We have to put all of our trust, hope, and faith in the Lord and bring our heart's desire to His throne. Although the Father already knows what we want and need, Job 22:27-28 states: *Thou shalt make thy prayer unto Him, and He shall hear thee, and thou shalt pay thy vows. Thou shalt also decree a thing, and it shall be established unto thee.*

Heaven is waiting for us to proclaim and obtain the inheritance of the sons and daughters of the Most High; then we can testify that *the Lord hath given me my petition which I asked of Him* (1 Samuel 1:27).

Inspired by the twelve tribes of Israel, here are some examples of common prayer requests:

TRIBE OF REUBEN

...THE BEGINNING OF MY STRENGTH... (GENESIS 49:3).

When you're feeling weak and you need some help to make it through, pray for...

STRENGTH

...And I was strengthened as the hand of the Lord my God was upon me... (Ezra 7:28).

He giveth power to the faint; and to them that have no might He increaseth strength...But they that wait upon the Lord shall renew their strength; they shall mount up with wings as eagles; they shall run, and not be weary; and they shall walk, and not faint (Isaiah 40:29, 31).

...My grace is sufficient for thee: for My strength is made perfect in weakness... (2 Corinthians 12:9).

I can do all things through Christ which strengtheneth me (Philippians 4:13).

41

*But if from thence thou shalt seek the Lord thy God,
thou shalt find Him, if thou seek Him with all thy
heart and with all thy soul (Deuteronomy 4:29).*

Use this page to record additional scriptures to pray.

_____

_____

_____

_____

_____

_____

_____

_____

_____

_____

_____

_____

_____

_____

_____

_____

_____

_____

_____

_____

_____

_____

_____

_____

_____

TRIBE OF SIMEON

...BECAUSE THE LORD HATH HEARD... (GENESIS 29:33).

If you're afraid or lonely and it looks like there's no one there to help you, pray for...

COURAGE

Be strong and of a good courage, fear not, nor be afraid of them: for the Lord thy God, He it is that doth go with thee; He will not fail thee, nor forsake thee (Deuteronomy 31:6).

...Be strong and of good courage, and do it: fear not, nor be dismayed: for the Lord God, even my God, will be with thee; He will not fail thee, nor forsake thee... (1 Chronicles 28:20).

I sought the Lord, and He heard me, and delivered me from all my fears (Psalm 34:4).

In righteousness shalt thou be established: thou shalt be far from oppression; for thou shalt not fear: and from terror; for it shall not come near thee (Isaiah 54:14).

This book of the law shall not depart out of thy
mouth; but thou shalt meditate therein
day and night... (Joshua 1:8).

Use this page to record additional scriptures to pray.

_____
_____
_____
_____
_____
_____
_____
_____
_____
_____
_____
_____
_____
_____
_____
_____
_____
_____
_____
_____
_____
_____
_____
_____
_____
_____

TRIBE OF LEVI

THEY SHALL TEACH ... ISRAEL THY LAW... (DEUTERONOMY 33:10).

Cover all those in authority - especially in your church, work and government - by praying for...

RIGHTEOUS LEADERS

...And they shall judge the people with just judgment. Thou shalt not wrest judgment; thou shalt not respect persons, neither take a gift: for a gift doth blind the eyes of the wise, and pervert the words of the righteous. That which is altogether just shalt thou follow... (Deuteronomy 16:18-20).

...He that ruleth over men must be just, ruling in the fear of God (2 Samuel 23:3).

Blessed is the man that walketh not in the counsel of the ungodly, nor standeth in the way of sinners, nor sitteth in the seat of the scornful (Psalm 1:1).

I exhort therefore, that, first of all, supplications, prayers, intercessions, and giving of thanks, be made for all men; For kings, and for all that are in authority; that we may lead a quiet and peaceable life in all godliness and honesty (1 Timothy 2:1-2).

Mine eyes prevent the night watches, that I might meditate in Thy Word (Psalm 119:148).

Use this page to record additional scriptures to pray.

_____

_____

_____

_____

_____

_____

_____

_____

_____

_____

_____

_____

_____

_____

_____

_____

_____

_____

_____

_____

_____

_____

TRIBE OF JUDAH

IN THOSE DAYS SHALL JUDAH BE SAVED... (JEREMIAH 33:16).

Decree and declare God's perfect plan for all the saints by praying for...

SALVATION

For God sent not his Son into the world to condemn the world; but that the world through him might be saved (John 3:17).

And it shall come to pass, that whosoever shall call on the name of the Lord shall be saved (Acts 2:21).

...Thou and all thy house shall be saved (Acts 11:14).

...The word of faith, which we preach; That if thou shalt confess with thy mouth the Lord Jesus, and shalt believe in thine heart that God hath raised him from the dead, thou shalt be saved. For with the heart man believeth unto righteousness; and with the mouth confession is made unto salvation (Romans 10:8-10).

47

The heart of the righteous
studieth to answer... (Proverbs 15:28)

Use this page to record additional scriptures to pray.

_____

_____

_____

_____

_____

_____

_____

_____

_____

_____

_____

_____

_____

_____

_____

_____

_____

_____

_____

_____

_____

_____

_____

TRIBE OF ZEBULUN

...HE SHALL BE FOR AN HAVEN OF SHIPS... (GENESIS 49:13).

When the floods come, the winds blow, and you feel like running away to escape, pray for...

PEACE

Great peace have they which love Thy law: and nothing shall offend them (Psalm 119:165).

Thou wilt keep him in perfect peace, whose mind is stayed on Thee: because he trusteth in Thee (Isaiah 26:3).

...Then He arose, and rebuked the wind and the raging of the water: and they ceased, and there was a calm (Luke 8:24).

And the peace of God, which passeth all understanding, shall keep our hearts and minds through Christ Jesus (Philippians 4:7).

And I gave my heart to seek and search out by wisdom concerning all things that are done under heaven... (Ecclesiastes 1:13).

Use this page to record additional scriptures to pray.

_____

_____

_____

_____

_____

_____

_____

_____

_____

_____

_____

_____

_____

_____

_____

_____

_____

_____

_____

_____

_____

_____

_____

_____

_____

TRIBE OF ISSACHAR

AND HE SAW...THE LAND THAT IT WAS PLEASANT... (GENESIS 49:15).

If you need something that can only be obtained through divine intervention, pray for...

PROVISION

Trust in the Lord, and do good; so shalt thou dwell in the land, and verily thou shalt be fed. Delight thyself also in the Lord; and He shall give thee the desires of thine heart. Commit thy way unto the Lord; trust also in Him; and He shall bring it to pass (Psalm 37:3-5).

...Yet have I not seen the righteous forsaken, nor his seed begging bread. He is ever merciful, and lendeth; and his seed is blessed (Psalm 37:25-26).

I will abundantly bless her provision: I will satisfy her poor with bread (Psalm 132:15).

But my God shall supply all your need according to His riches in glory by Christ Jesus (Philippians 4:19).

...Hearken diligently unto me, and eat ye that which is good, and let your soul delight itself in fatness (Isaiah 55:2).

Use this page to record additional scriptures to pray.

_____

_____

_____

_____

_____

_____

_____

_____

_____

_____

_____

_____

_____

_____

_____

_____

_____

_____

_____

_____

_____

_____

_____

_____

_____

TRIBE OF DAN

...GOD HATH JUDGED ME, AND HATH ALSO HEARD MY VOICE... (GENESIS 30:6).

Cover all that you've lost, all that you have, and all that God has promised you by praying for...

RESTORATION

Restore unto me the joy of Thy salvation; and uphold me with Thy free spirit (Psalm 51:12).

But if [the thief] be found, he shall restore sevenfold; he shall give all the substance of his house (Proverbs 6:31).

The glory of this latter house shall be greater than the of the former, saith the Lord of hosts: and in this place will I give peace, saith the Lord of hosts (Haggai 2:9).

The thief cometh not, but for to steal, and to kill, and to destroy: I am come that they might have life, and that they might have it more abundantly (John 10:10).

And ye shall seek Me, and find Me, when ye shall search for Me with all your heart. And I will be found of you, saith the Lord... (Jeremiah 29:13-14).

Use this page to record additional scriptures to pray.

_____
_____
_____
_____
_____
_____
_____
_____
_____
_____
_____
_____
_____
_____
_____
_____
_____
_____
_____
_____
_____
_____
_____
_____

TRIBE OF GAD

...BUT HE OVERCOME AT THE LAST (GENESIS 49:19).

Decree and declare wholeness and total recovery for all those who are ill by praying for...

HEALING

...If thou wilt diligently hearken to the voice of the Lord thy God, and wilt do that which is right in His sight, and wilt give ear to His commandments, and keep all His statues, I will put none of these diseases upon thee, which I have brought upon the Egyptians: for I am the Lord that healeth thee (Exodus 15:26).

O Lord my God, I cried unto Thee, and Thou hast healed me (Psalm 30:2).

...And with His stripes we are healed (Isaiah 53:5).

And the prayer of the faith shall save the sick, and the Lord shall raise him up; and if he have committed sins, they shall be forgiven him (James 5:15).

*Take My yoke upon you, and learn of Me; for I am
meek and lowly in heart: and ye shall find rest unto
your souls. For My yoke is easy,
and My burden is light (Matthew 11:29-30).*

Use this page to record additional scriptures to pray.

_____

_____

_____

_____

_____

_____

_____

_____

_____

_____

_____

_____

_____

_____

_____

_____

_____

_____

_____

_____

_____

TRIBE OF ASHER

...THE DAUGHTERS WILL CALL ME BLESSED... (GENESIS 30:13).

When you desire to bless others and want to be a good steward for the Lord, pray for...

PROSPERITY

For the Lord thy God blesseth thee, as He promised thee: and thou shalt lend unto many nations, but thou shalt not borrow... (Deuteronomy 15:6).

Honour the Lord with thy substance, and with the firstfruits of all thine increase: So shall thy barns be filled with plenty, and thy presses shall burst out with new wine (Proverbs 3:9-10).

Bring ye all the tithes into the storehouse...and prove me now herewith, saith the Lord of hosts, if I will not open you the windows of Heaven, and pour you out a blessing, that there shall not be room enough to receive it (Malachi 3:10).

Now He that ministereth seed to the sower, both minister bread for your food, and multiply your seed sown and increase the fruits of your righteousness (2 Corinthians 9:10).

...They received the Word with all readiness of mind and searched the scriptures daily... (Acts 17:11).

Use this page to record additional scriptures to pray.

_____

_____

_____

_____

_____

_____

_____

_____

_____

_____

_____

_____

_____

_____

_____

_____

_____

_____

_____

_____

_____

_____

TRIBE OF NAPHTALI

...HE GIVETH GOODLY WORDS (GENESIS 49:21).

If you want to be spiritually-minded and seek the counsel of the Almighty, pray for...

WISDOM

The fear of the Lord is the beginning of knowledge...My son, hear the instruction of thy father, and forsake not the law of thy mother (Proverbs 1:7-8).

Then shalt thou understand the fear of the Lord, and find the knowledge of God. For the Lord giveth wisdom: out of His mouth cometh knowledge and understanding. He layeth up sound wisdom for the righteous: He is a buckler to them that walk uprightly (Proverbs 2:5-7).

Trust in the Lord with all thine heart; and lean not unto thine own understanding. In all thy ways acknowledge Him, and He shall direct thy paths. Be not wise in thine own eyes: fear the Lord, and depart from evil (Proverbs 3:5-7).

Hear counsel, and receive instruction, that thou mayest be wise in the thy latter end (Proverbs 19:20).

*Meditate upon these things; give thyself wholly to them; that thy profiting
may appear to all (1 Timothy 4:15).*

Use this page to record additional scriptures to pray.

_____

_____

_____

_____

_____

_____

_____

_____

_____

_____

_____

_____

_____

_____

_____

_____

_____

_____

_____

_____

_____

_____

_____

_____

_____

_____

TRIBE OF JOSEPH

...A FRUITFUL BOUGH, EVEN A FRUITFUL BOUGH BY A WELL... (GENESIS 49:22).

Cover your spouse, children, and the future generations by praying for...

FAMILY COVENANT

...On this wise ye shall bless the children of Israel, saying unto them, The Lord bless thee, and keep thee: The Lord make his face shine upon thee, and be gracious unto thee: The Lord lift up his countenance upon thee, and give thee peace (Numbers 6:23-26).

...But as for me and my house, we will serve the Lord (Joshua 24:15).

Thy wife shall be as a fruitful vine by the sides of thine house: thy children like olive plants round about thy table. Behold, that thus shall the man be blessed that feareth the Lord (Psalm 128:3-4).

But from the beginning of the creation God made them male and female. For this cause shall a man leave his father and mother, and cleave to his wife; And they twain shall be one flesh: so then they are no more twain, but one flesh. What therefore God hath joined together, let not man put asunder (Mark 10:6-9).

Study to show thyself approved unto God, a workman that needeth not to be ashamed, rightly dividing the word of truth (2 Timothy 2:15).

Use this page to record additional scriptures to pray.

_____

_____

_____

_____

_____

_____

_____

_____

_____

_____

_____

_____

_____

_____

_____

_____

_____

_____

_____

_____

_____

_____

TRIBE OF BENJAMIN

...HE SHALL DEVOUR THE PREY AND ...DIVIDE THE SPOIL (GENESIS 49:27).

Decree and declare that the devil is a defeated foe and is now your footstool by praying for...

VICTORY

For the Lord your God is he that goeth with you, to fight for you against your enemies, to save you (Deuteronomy 20:4).

And all this assembly shall know that the Lord saveth not with sword and spear: for the battle is the Lord's... (1 Samuel 17:47).

No weapon that is formed against thee shall prosper; and every tongue that shall rise against thee in judgment thou shalt condemn. This is the heritage of the servants of the Lord, and their righteousness is of me, saith the Lord (Isaiah 54:17).

...When the enemy shall come in like a flood, the spirit of the Lord shall lift up a standard against him (Isaiah 59:19).

...He that cometh to God must believe that He is, and that He is a rewarder of them that diligently seek Him (Hebrews 11:6).

Use this page to record additional scriptures to pray.

_____

_____

_____

_____

_____

_____

_____

_____

_____

_____

_____

_____

_____

_____

_____

_____

_____

_____

_____

_____

_____

_____

_____

❤ LOVE ❤

LOVE suffereth long, and is kind; LOVE envieth not; LOVE vaunteth not itself, is not puffed up, Doth not behave itself unseemly, seeketh not her own, is not easily provoked, thinketh no evil; Rejoiceth not in iniquity, but rejoiceth in the truth; Beareth all things, believeth all things, hopeth all things, endureth all things. LOVE never faileth...And now abideth faith, hope, LOVE, these three; but the greatest of these is LOVE (1 Corinthians 13:4-8, 13).

"So what about love," you ask? Well, that's the one thing that you don't have to pray for because *God is love* (1 John 4:8)! That being said, at times you may have felt like I used to feel - that you're unlovable somehow because it seems that no one cares for you. My brothers and sisters, don't look to man for the things which your heavenly Father so freely gives to you - *For God so loved the world, that he gave his only begotten Son, that whosoever believeth in him should not perish, but have everlasting life* (John 3:16). And because the Lord loves us in such an unconditional way, He has the right to say to us today:

If My people, which are called by My name, shall humble themselves, and pray, and seek My face, and turn from their wicked ways; then will I hear from Heaven, and will forgive their sin, and will heal their land
(2 Chronicles 7:14).

Now unto the King eternal,
immortal, invisible,
the only wise God, be honour
and glory for ever and ever.
Amen (1 Timothy 1:17).

ACKNOWLEDGMENTS

Almighty God, you are my Father and my Creator. I give you praise and thanksgiving because with you, all things are possible. Jesus Christ, you are my Savior and my Redeemer. I give you praise and thanksgiving because I can do nothing without you. Holy Spirit, you are my Teacher and my Comforter. I give you praise and thanksgiving because you lead me and guide me into all truth.

I give honor and respect to every officer of the five-fold ministry and servant of God (He knows your names) who has taught me the Word and how to use it in prayer and spiritual warfare. Your labor of love will be rewarded.

I bless every prayer warrior and intercessor who takes their rightful position on the wall of salvation. Thank you for standing in unity to send the Word to every spirit-man in order for God's perfect will to be manifested in the earth.

I thank all of my spiritual brothers and sisters who obey God's voice and speak a word in season when I need it the most. We've been called to edify each other because we're all members of one body, and Christ is the head over us. His love is perfected in us when we love others.

And I must also thank my mother, Constance Blount, who made sure that we were at church <u>every</u> Sunday. You trained me up in the way that I should go, and I will not depart from it.

I love the Lord, because He hath heard my voice and my supplications. Because He hath inclined His ear unto me, therefore will I call upon Him as long as I live (Psalm 116:1-2).

14936558R00036

Made in the USA
Charleston, SC
09 October 2012